The Perfect Marriage
Marriage
HE Is Always Right

Melissa Templeman

Copyright © 2016 by Melissa Templeman

The Perfect Marriage
HE Is Always Right
by Melissa Templeman

Printed in the United States of America.

ISBN 9781498461702

All rights reserved solely by the author. The author guarantees all contents are original and do not infringe upon the legal rights of any other person or work. No part of this book may be reproduced in any form without the permission of the author. The views expressed in this book are not necessarily those of the publisher.

www.xulonpress.com

HE is always right

Good morning Mr. Right, I love it when you watch me sleep, or when I encounter you in my dreams. Taken a look back at waking up to all sorts of characters in previous books, I didn't know I wasn't supposed to love everyone that asked for my number, or thought I was cute, who knew this little girl just wanted a playmate from the beginning. Why do these boys always like to fight? Why don't they play fair? I'm a little girl and that hurts! Mom, am I supposed to hit back? Do I cry? Do these little boys want me to respond in their way? Am I angry at them or me? Am I out of control? So to keep me in line, I have to bow down, keep quiet, and take it as a little girl should............

Take Him Back

*H*ey mom and dad, hey honey, this is a little boy I found outside. Nice to meet you young man (young man?) is that when you speak things into existence? Anyway, can I keep him? (no, that's not what I asked them), but that's what I was thinking. Every time I would get a new boyfriend, I would change my last name on sheets of paper and draw all these types of heart and rainbows, and we would have kids and be happy. He would get on one knee and ask me to marry him, and we would be in love forever. WHOA, Stop IT! You're doing it again, drifting off. Hey, a girl has to dream right? He's perfect, He loves me and no one else right?..............

Stop Dreaming

I wake up from slumber and EEEEAAAAKKKK!!!!!!This is not what I was thinking of when I thought about marriage and kids, I had it all wrong. I didn't know I was going to get pregnant first and then get married, by shotgun or borrowing money to get the rings.(gold nugget rings, you remember those) the rings made it look like you have money, it was 14k, I thought I had hit the jackpot! Well at least walk around and try to look happy........ Why is he always hitting me, I thought we had the same dreams. He says he don't want anybody else (Yεy for me!) Where does all this anger comes from, his parents seem nice even though they are separated? Is this the new dream I'm living out...........

Wake UP

Wake up dear (mother in law says), you were sleeping so hard, Yeah I know I replied. In my mind I didn't want to wake up to this madness of a marriage, a crying baby and living with mom in law. Where is your nightmare of a son? (Of course I did not say that), but that's what is was. She said oh, he's out looking for a job. What?....You know, I'm going to get dressed and look for a job too. Can you watch the baby? Sure she said. (Hey I need a break too) that's what I was thinking. Maybe he won't come back so angry. Stop dreaming! I keep telling myself.........

We Need to Talk

Wake up dear (mother in law again), It seems you get the best sleep in the morning (Yea when nightmare leaves the house!) I didn't tell her this of course. So she said I have to tell you something, nightmares dad used to hit me too, that's why we are not together (now you tell me!). So I think you two should move and get your own place.(But I don't want him all to myself) (I didn't say that but...............)I really don't make enough money for our own place. She said I'll help you and him. I think she just wanted him out, just as much as I did. I'm thinking, when would I sleep? When he come back from robbing and stealing, getting buzzed like little boys that they are. Well this is too much good news in a day,(I was thinking). Time for me to go to work, maybe I'll run into my nightmare husband........................

Am I Married

Wake up honey! As I get punched in the leg, your baby is crying (My Baby?). Let me get up before he starts hitting him for no reason. Wait! Wait! He need a reason? Maybe he knows the baby can't fight back. Do he know I don't know how to fight back? I was not taught that in marriage one on one. Marriage? This is not the dream, I had ever since I was a little girl, noe I'm a big girl, mom in law said, and I'm supposed to hang in there for the good, the bad, and the ugly. How long do I wait for the good? Where's the forever love? When does the happy start? Where is my happy baby? Why do people have to wake me up? I don' like marriage, I don't like him, I don't like this angry baby. I don't like waking up!!!!!!!..............

New Dream

Hey I woke up on my own today. Wow that feels great! The baby is still sleeping, but where's nightmare? Oh okay, (as I look around the apartment), he didn't came home last night (GOOD)! I hope something happened to him(just Kidding.... am I?)What if he never come home? HHmm? Me and my baby will be just fine. It seems the baby doesn't cry as much when he's away and I don't either. It is so Peaceful here. Can I wake up every day like this? But that means he can't come home every night, that's not marriage. So when your husband don't come home, that's good right? Do I fix him breakfast, because that's what a good wife do...... right? Where is he? Is he alive? He's probably buzzed.........

You First

As I prepare for this big day, I wasn't getting the feelings I thought I was going to have, I thought I was going to have a big wedding, you know the white dress and my dad walking me down the aisle, my mom in the pews crying tears of joy, come home to a picket fence and watch our family grow. As reality set in, never knowing that you LORD was first to walk down the aisle, with your Crown of thorns on your head, suffering all that pain for me. I didn't know what LOVE looked like, I didn't know it was another way, no one told me you were going to be walking down the aisle of DEATH, and it was ALL PLANNED by your FATHER. Now I get it. That's why I'm getting up, putting on my jeans and a shirt and he had the same on, so his mom let us use the car and we went to the courthouse and my parents went to work. No celebration, no honeymoon, just plain ole broke! No rings, I need a drink and Not Wine, maybe that will help me forget this day. I don't want to remember every year that goes by. Can it get any worse? No more dreams of white dresses and such. This is not going to end well. LORD how did you do it?..........................

Reality Show

Hey, as he walks in from being out all night. Hey (me talking), where have you been? He said, oh hanging with the fellas, so I'm thinking to myself......I don't want to talk about nothing, my soap operas about to come on, before I go to work, that's my escape from this madness. Everybody is married, and cheating on each other, big diamond rings, big houses, money flowing everywhere. That's the life, except for the cheating part, because I'm no cheater......not yet anyways......There I go again thinking out loud! Come here and give me a kiss. I was thinking YUCK!! I don't know where you've been, but to keep the peace, YucK! Here, now can I watch T.V. before I go to work. I wish I had someone to talk to other than his mother (who thinks this abusive marriage is okay). I hope I meet someone at work and they could buy me a drink afterwards, you know before I get home. Day in and day out I don't know what to expect when I get home. It's funny how no one gets drunk on T.V. They are all controlled and stuff. Me, I want it all, you know keep my glass full, so I could forget all the foolishness around me. Look at me already planning the end of my shift. Already buzzed when I leave work. This is the life..........right?...........

Show Me

*L*ord, why being alone is the best, I can think, I can talk to you all day long, whenever I want. You are never wrong, we don't argue, you don't hit me when I mess up. All you do is forgive and forget and wipe the slate clean every day. This is marriage right here, the unconditional love. Walking down the aisle with you is everything. Finally dying to self and giving you my all, knowing you will never leave me or forsake me. Knowing you will protect and guide me all the way through, to the end. Always have kind words speaking to me and over me. Knowing our kids will be well, rich in goodness you provide. Rich in Mercy and Grace. All these years I've been waiting on you Mr. Right, never seeing you, but knowing you are here, and everywhere I go. Take me in your loving arms. Don't tell me again how much you love me (just kidding). You tell me every day, and you shoe me. You know I cry every time you tell me you love me (of course you do). I get chills and shakes like every married woman get..........right? Should I tell them or keep this secret to myself, will my friends understand what we have? And they could have it too. Are they ready to die? To self? Are they willing to give it all up? Or do they think they can do it all by themselves. Do they know who they are? Some of their lives is like these reality shows (always drama), and have built their marriage around the fake, plastic, lies the T.V. created. Not looking towards the Creator for help. I'm going to tell them who my heart belongs to (and its safe), and HE is my everything, HE fills every void in my life, there is no other, and when I said I do, HE said it's Done! He said I will take you places you never been before. I Love you Mr. Right, I'm All In!

Back To Work

Good morning, my boss said, hello I replied, but it's in the afternoon, he doesn't know how my morning was like (angry, didn't want to wake up, regrets, wondering why I'm alive) you know the usual. I'm already thinking how can I get some money to get drunk before I get home to nightmare, or maybe call my coworker to see if I could work there shift, so I don't have to go home at all. That will be great, not going home (YES!). How's the baby my boss asked. OH he's fine (when he's quiet). I didn't say that (customer walks in). Hi, he said and I replied hi, can I help you. Yeah, he said, by giving me your number (that's smooth) (not) excuse me? I see you a lot around here, what's your name? My name is married, what's yours? I replied, he said married too! But I'm not happy, well me too. I can't give you my number, nightmare is going to answer the phone. Well, give me the number here at your job. Oh okay, (wow is that a smile on my face). Yes we need to talk about why are we so unhappy and why this feels so right. Wow, it amazes me why I'm so quick to pick up strangers and have more to talk about than my own husband. Well at least he's older and I can get some wisdom from him.(Wow) the phone is ringing. Hello (I'm thinking did he get out of the parking lot?). Hey he said, I was seeing if this was a fake number (I'm thinking pressed), yeah I'm old school, and we used to say things like that. I couldn't afford a cell phone (I would really be in trouble). Can I take you out some time he said, I don't know, you would have to take me out of this area, my nightmare is usually stalking me as soon as I get off work. (YUK!).That's fine, how are we going to do this? I don't know, I said. I was sitting there day dreaming, hoping he would pick me up and I never come back, Hmm, who would take care of the baby? Nightmare? (YUK!) Nightmares mom? My mom? Well he is just going to have to accept me and baby. Wait! Wait? You have four kids (wow), (he must be a good catch). Why is he unhappy? Oh, she doesn't understand you like to cheat. (I didn't say that), but you know I was thinking it. Hmm and now I'm about to cheat on my husband. I need a drink, because right now I don't care If I get caught or not. I hate nightmare so much, I want to be with anybody for attention. You know the good attention, when no one is hitting you and or verbally abusing you, calling you all kinds of names that don't agree with my Spirit. I know me and married man are going to leave our spouses and live happily ever after right?....... I need a plan! There I go again jumping the gun, I don't even know his last name. I just want a loving man to put his arms around me and tell me he loves me and call me by my real name,(what I was born with). As long as he doesn't hit me, we will be okay. I just want to be rescued. You know like the soap operas. Wow eight hours flew, now I don't mind going home, I can't' wait till tomorrow, when married man calls. There I go again smiling for all the wrong reasons. Let me borrow off my check to get something to drink (you could do this back in the day). I have to be numb, by the time I get home (which is five minutes away). I never know what to expect on a day to day in my household. Yeah, I'll take a twelve pack. I hope married man drinks, then we would have something else in common, other than two lonely people, that is trying to escape from the mess at home. (CHEERS!).

Dear GOD

Thank you LORD for saving me from all the mess I created. I'm back home getting a divorce from nightmare, I and baby are fine (but you already know that). I haven't slept so good in years, I'm glad mom and dad said I can come back home, and get myself together. I'm going to tell you right now that I don't know where to begin. I need you, show me how to love myself, how to love this baby, how to forgive nightmare, how to forgive married man for hitting me! (Yeah he hit me also and was an alcoholic just like me. But I had an excuse, I drank for protection, I don't know why he drank. I'm glad you removed me from that bad situation, and it could have been worse. I know it's has to be worst for married man's wife, she has to be miserable. What I know now is never I mean never mess with a married man or boy.(Some men are just plain greedy!), they want it all and someone else's. Now i have some laws in place, no married men, no hitting, and no alcoholics, now I know want I want in a man, and they better accept my baby.. Lord I just want Peace, I can do it if I stick to the laws

The Perfect Marriage

of little girl. Lord can I be happy by myself? Probably not, I never heard of that, I've never been by myself, I've always had a boy and a man boy in my life, I know that sounds crazy, but I'm a girl, not a woman yet. You know having a baby and a husband doesn't make you a grown up. I need guidance, now where am I going to get that? I don't know your voice yet, I can't hear from you in between drinks. I know you have a lot to tell me, but I'm not ready. Can you tell someone to tell me (I seem to listen to anybody for advice), mostly my friends and they are silly like me. What went wrong in that nightmare of a marriage? I'm still angry, I lost so much time with him and the married man. I hope my baby don't be mad at me for spending so much time with negative people (it almost killed us). Lord, I know you have a plan for me, can you just lay it out all for me, so I can understand. But how will I know it's you? Oh well, the next man I get, I'm going to ask him, do you go to church? Because maybe he will teach me something or know more than me, because right now, all I know is that there is a GOD, and it's not a girl's intuition, that six sense, men think we got. Lord send me somebody that loves me like you love me (is that even possible?). In the meantime, I'm going to do my own searching for Mr. Right.

Signed Lonely Wife.

New Relationship

It's been a long time since we talked, LORD, I've been in a ten year relationship that was going nowhere. I thought I could change him, but in the end he changed me. I should have listen, two years into the relationship, you told me that was not my husband! You were very clear and I heard your voice, I thought since me and you had a relationship, I could talk you into giving him to me. He had so many good qualities for one he was not married, he did not hit me, he loved my baby and I end up having a baby by him, which he loved also. He just wasn't the one for me, I'm glad me and him can still be friends (now that's growing up!). So I'm still lonely with two kids. I know I'm supposed to me married, it's going to be hard trying to find a man that wants me and two kids. Well let me add another law,(he can't have kids) I know that sounds selfish, but I don't have time for baby mama drama, I hear too many stories about exes and kids and don't forget money. I want to move away from here and start all over. Well my oldest is going to live with his nightmare of a father. I told him I don't think it's a good idea, because his dad has some issues, he has to deal with. But he said mom I'm going to be okay, I need to get to know him (good luck), that's what I was thinking. I never told him about the abuse. I knew eventually it was going to come out, but if he ask me I'm going to tell him when he is old enough. (You know 18 or If I think he could handle the truth. I just don't want him walking in the same shoes as his dad, I don't want him disrespecting girls or woman or anybody. I wander do he know the difference between girls and woman? I'm going to tell him all about girls and women, but first I have to tell him all about the Lord. Can I call you Mr. RIGHT? Can I call you my ALLWAYS. I've noticed when I'm sober I can talk to you all night, and you are always here to listen, and tell me your innermost thoughts. I feel honored when talk to you. You mean I could have had this all along? Where Have I been? Where has the time gone? Thank you for never leaving me or forsaking me. Thank you for forgiving me and letting me hit those life lessons the hard way, I hear you Lord, but I'm not ready to be all Holy and stuff, I still like my beer. Hey, I met somebody new. He helped me and my daughter move. I know I haven't changed, I'm still looking for Love or just a companion. I don't need a relationship with him (he's too silly), and he don't have too much to offer, but neither do I. I guess it will be okay for right now till I meet someone else.

Why Me?

Hi, he said, I replied hi, what's your name, he said they call me disappearing act. Oh okay, they call me lonely wife. I can move your stuff for little to nothing at all, that's great (not knowing he had his own agenda). So most of the evening went past, we sat back and told each other everything the other wanted to hear, so he stayed the night in my new apartment (Don't Judge Me!) and anyway that's what girls do. We have unprotected sex with boys, we don't know. I didn't know I was supposed to save myself for marriage (you see where that went) just saying. We supposed to get to know them, then ask them about their past, then meet the parents and so on. Well I'll just play the game, like girls do. Well at least he doesn't have kids, because I just can't take him seriously, I don't know if he's telling me the truth or not. It's hard getting to know somebody when there past is just as ugly as yours. Should I tell him? Can this boy handle my mess (I can barely). Knock Knock at the door, (a couple of month has past) hey, he said, I replied where have you been, oh I forgot, you like to disappear, well anyway I'm late, he said late for what? (Isn't he silly), you know I didn't say that. I'm late for my cycle for this month. He said I'll be right back, I'm going to get a pregnancy test. Make sure you come back! (Telling time is not your gift) as I laughed to myself. So he came back hours later of course, I had just finished a whole bottle of champagne, that he had left in the fridge.(Yum). So I had to go to the bathroom anyways, you know what happened next right.....Yes, I'm pregnant again. I'm too old for this and you, I said. I already know you are not ready, but I'm glad anyway. So as disappearing act showed up from time to time, we are growing further and further apart. I just don't know what he wants from me. He talks like he wants a family, but shows me something completely different. I'm so tired of all the lies and games we are both playing. Lord if he's not good for us, send him away. So for five years, he was in and out of our lives and I was okay with it. But in between those years I was still drinking and trying to find Mr. Right......................

Last Call for Alcohol

*G*ood morning Lord, it seems your starting to move people and things out of the way. I heard you say STOP drinking for forty days. I said this has to be you Lord, because I still want to drink, but I will do it, because you scare me!(in a good way)....so I did it, my mind got so clear, I was on the right track. As my daily talk with you Lord, we were building something, I can't describe it, it was a Love so deep, and that was inside me the whole time. You told me things about myself, that I didn't know, you told me you Love me, you showed me thing that no one ever showed me, you told me who I was, and WHO's I was, you told me you were going to deliver me (which you did). You said you will sustain me, that I would not have to look any further. I will fill all those voids in your life. Stop running away from ME, run towards Me. Get to know ME and all the plans I have for you and your husband (MY WHAT?). YES your husband. Can you tell me who it is? Yes, the Lord said, its disappearing act, AND STOP CALLING MY SON THAT! Yes Lord, forgive me. Lord I don't know your son let alone love him. I KNOW. Lord you have to show me how to Love like you, forgive like you, Honor like you, respect like you. Thank you Lord for finding me and saving me. Now I know how a man supposed to Love a woman and vise-versa. I didn't know you had a plan all along. Thank you for walking me down the aisle. I SURRENDER........................

LOVE, MRS.

Milton Keynes UK
Ingram Content Group UK Ltd.
UKHW050625210324
439796UK00013B/1093